Easter

Program
Book

Number 36

compiled by
Laurie Hoard

cover photo by
Fred Sieb

STANDARD PUBLISHING
Cincinnati, Ohio   8704

ISBN 0-87239-870-6

CONTENTS

Easter

Recitations
  Easy   5
  Medium   7
  Difficult   13

Exercises   23

Programs   25

Mother's Day

Recitations   34

Exercises   39

Father's Day

Recitations   44

Exercises   48

Easy

HERE I AM

Helen Kitchell Evans

Here I am this Easter
Thankful as can be,
Thankful for the blessings
My Lord has given me.

NOT VERY BIG

Robert Colbert

I'm not so very big,
I'm not so very tall,
But I can say for sure
That Jesus died for all.

WHY FLOWERS BLOOM

Helen Kitchell Evans

God makes the flowers bloom
So all of us can see
How wonderful He is,
And how He loves you and me.

*(Point to self and then congregation
on "you and me.")*

MY FRIEND

Edith Hafley

Jesus is my Savior,
Jesus is my friend.
I'll love Him forever,
To the very end.

LOVELY MORNING

Helen Kitchell Evans

Easter bells are joyful,
I am happy, too;
On this lovely morning
May I welcome you.

*(Extends hands toward congregation,
bows slightly.)*

WHAT THEY SAY

Phyllis Michael

The birds are sweetly singing,
Easter bells are ringing;
And here is what they say,
"Jesus lives today."

AREN'T YOU HAPPY?

Helen Kitchell Evans

Aren't you happy at Easter?
It's such a wonderful day,
Because Jesus rose from the grave,
And the stone was rolled away.

HAPPY EASTER DAY

Antoinette Niederberger

We've sung about our Savior,
And heard the lessons, too.
Today we're celebrating Easter.
I'm very glad, aren't you?

WHEN YOU ARE THREE

Helen Kitchell Evans

When you are three
What do you say?
Hope you have
A nice Easter Day.

SOMETHING TO TELL YOU

Phyllis Michael

I can't do much for Jesus
But *S M I L E,*
And tell you folks you're welcome
  here,
As welcome as can be.

(One child recites and five other children appear one by one and stand beside the child reciting. Each child carries a letter to spell "Smile." The word need not be spoken.)

WONDERFUL DAY

Helen Kitchell Evans

It's Easter, it's Easter,
  It's wonderful spring;
"Wake up, wake up,"
  Hear all the birds sing.

Spread joy in the world!
  There are kind words to say.
So, love one another
  On this beautiful day.

NO MATTER

Phyllis Michael

Boys and girls, girls and boys,
  God loves us one and all.
And we should always love Him, too,
  No matter how big or small.

HE LIVES

Antoinette Niederberger

Jesus lives within my heart;
  He takes away my fear.
If we trust Him all our days
  He is always near.

I FOOLED EVERYONE

Helen Kitchell Evans

(Child peeks to left behind sign.)
Bet you thought I couldn't;

(Peeks to right from behind sign.)
Mother thought I wouldn't,

(Stands straight and tall.)
I'm glad that I can say,
I fooled everyone, I guess,
By standing here today.

*(Child carries a sign with "**Happy Easter**" printed on it. The sign remains with words toward child until the last when it is turned toward the congregation and held high over the child's head as he leaves the platform.)*

EASTER SUNDAY

Edith Hafley

We shouldn't worship Jesus
  Just on Easter Day.
He doesn't pick a special time
  To send His love our way.
Jesus' love is constant,
  And so it should be with us.
We should love Him daily,
  With all our love and trust.

HELLO OUT THERE!

Helen Kitchell Evans

I'm a little messenger
  Here to do my share;
Let me think a minute,
(Pauses, hand to chin.)
  Oh! Hello out there!
(Extends arms with a fling to congregation.)

Medium

HE IS RISEN
Nona Keen Duffy

Though they hung Him on a cross
  In the heat and glare,
Be still and turn within
  And you will find Him there!

Though they laid Him in a tomb,
  And many tears were shed,
Let the earth be full of joy;
  He is risen, as He said!

NEW LIFE
Helen Kitchell Evans

Vibrant and true ring out the bells
  On this beautiful Easter Day;
Praise God in Heaven up above,
  For the stone was rolled away!

Everywhere we see new life;
  In the flowers, in blades of grass,
In the warming sun upon us,
  In the robins that we pass.

New life, a new beginning!
  Praise God we are alive!
A time to renew our faith,
  Old ambitions to revive.

WITHOUT JESUS
Edith Hafley

Did you ever stop to think what this life
  would be
If God had not sent Jesus to die for
  you and me?
If we had no salvation, and no one to
  pray to,
Life would be so meaningless for me,
  and yes, for you.
For without Jesus we are lost as a
  ship upon the sea
That has no light to follow, and knows
  not its destiny.

EASTER TIME
Nona Keen Duffy

It's time now for Easter,
  And bells to ring;
For anthems and lilies,
  And birds that sing!

The field's full of color;
  A bird up above
Is singing, expressing
  A heart full of love!

It's time now for Easter.
  Rejoice in the Lord,
For Jesus is risen
  And by us adored!

A SPRING MORNING

Helen Kitchell Evans

The beauty of blossom-time
 All along the way;
Down the garden path
 Purple lilacs greet the day.

Apricot azaleas spread
 A glow upon the grass;
Everywhere perfume greets me
 As I slowly pass.

I thank God for the beauty
 Of what the seasons bring,
Especially this morning
 For the loveliness of spring.

HELP ME TO REMEMBER

Antoinette Niederberger

Help me to remember
 The great joy He gives,
Guiding us each moment,
 Triumphantly He lives.

Help me to remember
 Our future Heav'nly home,
That we may be with Him
 Because of love He's shown.

ANGEL ROLLED THE STONE

Nona Keen Duffy

An angel rolled the stone away
Upon that first glad Easter Day!
And Christ stood up from borrowed
 tomb,
Triumphant over death and doom.
 Praise God for deathless love!

When Mary came at break of day
She found the stone was rolled away;
She saw the Christ in robe of white
Triumphant over death and night!
 Praise God who reigns above!

HE ALONE

Helen Kitchell Evans

We can never earn our way
 Into Heaven by our deeds;
But God has made it possible,
 And He will satisfy our needs.

He has done for each of us
 What we could never do;
Upon the cross He gave himself
 That we have life anew.

He alone can forgive our sins,
 And help us through days of strife;
Only our Lord and Savior
 Can give us eternal life.

8

WE COME TODAY
Phyllis Michael

We come today with singing
  And very good news to say,
Like Mary, we've been told
  The stone was rolled away.

We come today rejoicing,
  We know that Jesus lives;
And, oh, what peace and gladness
  This news forever gives.

EASTER
Nona Keen Duffy

This is the time of lilies
  When the season is at its dawn;
This is the time of sprouting,
  For winter and darkness are gone!

This is a time of resurgence,
  For reviewing and mending our
  ways,
A time for resurrection,
  For lifting up and praise!

NO NEED FOR FEAR
Helen Kitchell Evans

He is risen—hallelujah!
  He is not among the dead!
Because of Him, the end of life
  There is no need to dread.

Our hope has been rekindled,
  For He is ever near;
Because Christ lives
  He conquered all our fear.

THE EASTER LILY
Phyllis Michael

Each flower that grows is a pretty
  thing,
  But I like the lily best;*
It's pure and white and blooms each
  spring,
  This I'm sure you've guessed.

But then there's another very good
  reason,
It's because it reminds me, too,
Of what Jesus did that Easter season
Long ago for me and you.

(Child points to a lily.)

THE FIRST EASTER
Nona Keen Duffy

How joyful Jesus must have been
  That first, glad Easter Day,
When He could lay the shroud aside
  And slowly walk away!

Jesus triumphed over death
  And cruelty and grief;
He forgave all ignorance,
  All scorn and unbelief!

He must have felt our Father's love
  And heard a glad, "Well done!
You have paid the final debt,
  My own, beloved Son!"

Jesus overcame the world,
  He banished doubt and gloom;
He triumphed over sin and death,
  And rose up from the tomb!

THE DAWN OF EASTER

Antoinette Niederberger

The day was dark at Calvary
  When He was on the tree.
The morning was bright with sun-
shine,
  Glistening for the world to see.

Our dear Savior rose to Heaven
  And is with His Father above.
So we must tell the story
  Of His wonderful, saving love.

WHEN I THINK OF EASTER

Nona Keen Duffy

When I think of Easter
  I think of candlelight,
Of Sunday school and singing,
  Of choirs robed in white.

I think of church and flowers
  And of a ringing bell,
Of Mary in the morning,
  And Him we love so well.

It makes me think of angels
  Who rolled the stone away,
And Jesus, who was living
  On that first Easter Day!

AN EASTER DAY OF CHEER

Helen Kitchell Evans

Springtime is like a song
  That floats softly through the air;
The breeze, the flowers, the rain-
drops—
  There is such joy everywhere.

Every bud and leaf gives us
  An Easter Day of cheer,
Bringing blessings from above
  To all of us right here.

I'VE PRACTICED

Helen Kitchell Evans

Looking at me
  I can hear you say,
"What can (he or she) do
  On Easter Day?

Well, don't be surprised
  At how well I can do;
I've practiced really hard
  To get before you!

HAPPY EASTER!

GETHSEMANE

Antoinette Niederberger

Before the morn of Easter
  There was a garden called
  Gethsemane.
Before Christ rose to Heaven
  There were hours of agony.
And when I take my burdens to God
  Let my prayer be as God's Son,
That night in dark Gethsemane:
  "Thy will, not mine, be done."

EASTER MESSAGE

Nona Keen Duffy

Easter bells are gaily ringing
  From the tower high above;
Hear the message they are bringing,
  "God is love! God is love!"

Choirs in church are sweetly singing,
  And their praise ascends above;
Hear the message they are bringing,
  "God is love! God is love!"

ALL YEAR THROUGH

Helen Kitchell Evans

God made the birds
  That nest in trees;
He made the flowers
  And a summer breeze.

God made everything
  For each one of you;
Let's be happy this Easter
  And all the year through.

BECAUSE OF LOVE

Antoinette Niederberger

Because of love my Jesus died;
For you and me, He was crucified.
Because of love He came to live
Upon this earth, His life to give.
Because of love He lives today
In my heart, this Easter Day.

THE FIRST EASTER

Nona Keen Duffy

Upon that first
  Glad Easter Day,
An angel rolled
  The stone away!

Then Jesus stood
  In robes of white,
Triumphant over
  Death and night.

The birds were gay
  On happy wings,
The flowers and trees
  Were dancing things!

The women kneeled
  To softly pray,
For Christ arose
  On Easter Day!

GOD IS NEAR

Helen Kitchell Evans

Whether it's a small church
  Or a big one somewhere,
When Easter Day arrives
  There is joy in the air.

Hallelujah! It is Easter!
  Every choir will sing,
And God is very near us
  When Easter bells ring.

BIRDS CAN TALK

Helen Kitchell Evans

Did you know that birds can talk?
   Well, one talked to me today
As I was on my way to church;
   This is what I heard him say,
"Be glad, be glad, be glad,
   Be glad, be glad, and sing,
For Jesus lives forever.
   He is our Lord, our King!"

SPRING MEANS HAPPY EASTER

Helen Kitchell Evans

*(To the tune of "Bringing in the
Sheaves.)*

When the birds are singing,
When the flowers are blooming,
When the grass is greener,
Then we know it's spring.

When the sun is shining,
When the clouds are climbing,
We are all rejoicing,
For we know it's spring.

Yes, we know it's spring,
Yes, we know it's spring,
We are all rejoicing,
For we know it's spring.

Spring means Happy Easter,
   Happy Easter Day,
When our Lord and Savior
   Rolled the stone away!

SETBACKS NEED NOT DEFEAT

Helen Kitchell Evans

Lord, the cross for You
   Was far worse than I may ever
   bear;
Your suffering was greater—
   For us, nothing can compare.

Thank You for Your example
   Of how we must face life;
Through all the joys and sorrows,
   Through all victory and strife.

Setbacks need never defeat us,
   We know the victory can be won
When our minds are fixed on Jesus,
   The gift of God's only Son.

EASTER'S MESSAGE

Helen Kitchell Evans

In springtime how clearly
   Is God's glory revealed,
For tiny flowers peep through
   Where once they were concealed.

It's nature's Easter message
   For all of us to see,
As we celebrate the resurrection
   Of our Christ from Calvary.

Easter's story is triumphant,
   Every heart is filled with love,
As we receive the Easter blessing
   From our Father up above.

CLOSING

Helen Kitchell Evans

May you be happy this Easter,
   And each day the whole year
   through;
Please come back again next year
   So I can welcome you!

Difficult

ON THAT EARLY SUNDAY MORNING

Henry Webb

On that early Sunday morning
 In the garden long ago,
Was Christ's almighty miracle
 That all the world must know.
On that early Sunday morning
 As the day began to dawn,
There came the dawn of mighty truth
 And doubts and fears were gone.

"Why seek the living 'mongst the
 dead?"
 Made sense to those who came,
As fact and faith transformed their
 cries
 To "Blessed be His name!"
He proved His victory over death;
 Eternal life—the key,
His Holy Spirit's power to save
 The likes of you and me.

He made it plain what He had done
 Could not apply, you see,
'Till my repentant faith obeyed
 His plan to ransom me.
"Deny—forsake—take up thy cross—
 Be crucified with me."
For only to the crucified
 Can resurrection be!

Without the resurrection
 The cross is all in vain.
Without the cross and His shed blood
 No gospel to proclaim.
Regeneration—quickening power
 To usward who believe;
The same God wrought in Jesus
 Christ,
 The risen Lord receive.

Since now with Christ I'm risen
 My affections are above;
Since I have therefore received Him,
 I am walking in His love.
For I witness now with power
 How He died to set me free,
But with greater power I witness
 How He's living now in me.

Now on every waking morning
 As this pilgrim's way I go,
There's a joyful expectation
 That just sets my heart aglow.
For I know I shall be like Him,
 Resurrection glory know,
Like that early Sunday morning
 In the garden long ago.

13

PALM SUNDAY

Nona Keen Duffy

If I had lived
When Jesus lived
And taught in the
    Holy Land,
I would have been
A herald of His
And joined the
    children's band!
I would have sung
A hosanna for Him,
And carried a palm branch
    High in my hand!

"Hosanna! Hosanna!
The King is come!
He enters the city!
- He's passing by;
Spread greens for His feet,
Sing songs for His ears,
Cut branches of palm leaves
    And hold up high!"

VICTORY

Helen Kitchell Evans

The day was hot and sunny,
    The cries of adoration were loud
As the procession gathered
    And moved forward through the
    crowd.

The towers and domes of Jerusalem
    Gleamed in the morning sun
As Jesus, the king, rode a donkey,
    Jesus, God's only beloved Son.

"Blessed is He who comes in the
    name of the Lord!"
Jesus accepted the cheer.
But there were others along the way
    Who stood bewildered and in fear.

There were those who waved the
    palm branches,
    There were enemies who were up-
    set;
"Behold the whole world is gone after
    Him,
    And we've done nothing yet."

This was a victorious day for Jesus,
    But His message was not complete;
It was the day of resurrection
    That placed believers at His feet.

THE STONE HAS BEEN ROLLED AWAY

Helen Kitchell Evans

Have we hid behind a stone of guilt,
    Allowed ourselves to decay?
It's time to become alive and see
    The stone has been rolled away!

Has our conscience kept us in bond-
    age,
    Fearing we might others betray?
It's time to become alive and see
    The stone has been rolled away!

Have we been unable to release
    A habit that caused us to stray?
It's time to become alive and see
    The stone has been rolled away!

Has grief over lack of love in our loves
    Brought sadness to every day?
It's time to become alive and see
    The stone has been rolled away!

Let the dawn of Easter morning
    A true meaning to us convey;
It's time to become alive and see
    The stone has been rolled away!

THE FIRST EASTER
Nona Keen Duffy

Jesus hung upon the cross
  With thorns upon His head,
Because His speech offended some
  He suffered and He bled!

Jesus hung upon the cross
  With spear thrusts in His side;
He prayed for those who hated Him,
  Then ceased to breathe, and died!

Jesus lay within a tomb
  With bloodstains on His head;
Three days and nights His body lay,
  Then rose up from the dead!

Jesus rose up from the tomb
  And then He walked away;
Because He triumphed over death
  We commemorate, today!

EASTER
Nona Keen Duffy

Jesus lay within a tomb
  With spear thrusts in His side;
Far and near the people heard
  That Jesus Christ had died!

Jesus slept within a tomb
  And triumphed as He lay;
He breathed again and angels came
  And pushed the stone away!

Jesus lay within a tomb
  Thorn pricks upon His head;
Three days and nights He rested there
  Then rose up from the dead!

Jesus rose up from the tomb
  And then He walked away;
Because He triumphed over death
  We celebrate, today!

NEVER ALONE
Helen Kitchell Evans

Loneliness can be
  Filled with grief and pain,
But recall Gethsemane
  And how Jesus rose again.

Jesus shrank from the humiliation
  And death He was to face;
But through prayer He had the strength
  When given God's true grace.

As we face anxieties
  And fears we all have known,
Let us ever remember
  That we're never really alone.

15

THE MORNING OF EASTER

Helen Kitchell Evans

It was early the morning of Easter
  When a few of the frightened, afraid,
Quietly walked to the tomb of our Lord
  To again see the place He was laid.

In amazement they stood there bewildered,
  For they found the huge stone rolled away;
Then an angel called to them, "He has risen!
  He has risen on this Easter Day!"

"He has risen!" they cried as they hurried
  To tell others what the angel had said;
They shouted to all that would listen,
  "Our dear Savior is no longer dead!"

Almost two thousand years have passed,
  But the message today is so real
That we find ourselves there at the tomb,
  Knowing just how those present would feel.

What a message this Easter Day brings!
  Over evil the vict'ry was won,
And our God up in Heaven has given
  To His people the gift of His Son.

EASTER AGAIN

Nona Keen Duffy

Life is a cycle
  That must be reborn;
The buds are now swelling,
  And we're planting the corn.

New calves and wee lambkins
  Arrive every day;
The piglets are rooting
  Around in the hay.

Chickies are hatching,
  Lilies unfold;
Tulips appear
  That are yellow as gold!

From a dark tomb
  Jesus burst through;
This glad Easter Day
  He is born anew!

From selves we've outgrown,
  Again we are born
To arise with the Christ
  This bright Easter morn!

EASTER

Nona Keen Duffy

How joyful Jesus must have been
 That first glad Easter Day
When the angel laid the shroud aside
 And rolled the stone away!

He must have felt our Father's love
 And heard Him say, "Well done;
You now have overcome the world,
 My own beloved Son!"

"You've comforted the lonely ones,
 And healed the sick and lame;
You've given vision, hope, and love
 All in your Father's name!"

How joyful Jesus must have felt
 When trials were passed away,
To feel himself at peace with God,
 That first glad Easter Day!

LET MANKIND REJOICE

Helen Kitchell Evans

Easter is a day of glory,
 Darkness disappears;
Light floods over all the earth
 Dispelling all our fears.

Spirits are resurrected,
 Hope is born anew;
We seem to come alive
 When the cross we view.

Easter penetrates the gloom,
 With praise lift your voice;
As Christ has overcome the world,
 Let mankind rejoice!

IT'S FRIDAY

Helen Kitchell Evans

It's Friday, Good Friday, my friend,
 A day of darkness over all the land;
But wait! Sunday is coming,
 All will be gloriously grand.

It's Friday, the day Jesus was denied
 By all of His very close friends;
But wait! Sunday is coming
 With joy that never ends.

It's Friday, the day Jesus was rejected,
 All called for His execution;
But wait! Sunday is coming
 With God's promised solution.

It's Friday and Jesus is in the tomb,
 But we do not weep in vain;
For Sunday He will arise.
Let all the world praise His name!

THE RESURRECTION

Nona Keen Duffy

The angel said, "Don't be afraid,
See the place where He was laid.
I know you seek the One who died,
He was nailed to a cross and cruci-
 fied.

"He is not here, He is not dead,
For He has risen, as He said;
Come, see the place where Jesus lay,
He has risen up this day.

"Then quickly go and tell His friends
That He has risen and the mourning
 ends;
He is going before you to Galilee,
Lo, I have told you, go and see!"

READY FOR EASTER

Nona Keen Duffy

The world is getting all decked out
　In beauty and in style;
The earth is green and bright and
　clean,
　And wears a pleasant smile!
The purple lilac has unfurled
　In bouquet-scented gown;
The tulips have the gayest hats
　Of anyone in town!

The apple tree looks fresh and young
　In dress of petal pink;
The trees are getting greener leaves,
　For Easter Day, I think!
The lovely fragrant hyacinths
　And yellow daffodils
Have dainty ruffled petticoats
　With narrow, fluted frills.

The daisy, growing by the brook,
　Is graceful, tall, and slim;
She wears a hat with golden crown
　And tilted petal brim.
The earth is all reborn, again,
　And joy has come to stay,
Because our Christ rose from a tomb
　And triumphed, Easter Day!

EASTER UNFOLDS

Helen Kitchell Evans

God in His infinite goodness
　Brings newness of life in the spring;
He spreads out a mantle of green
　And the birds make their messages
　ring.

All trees send forth tiny leaves,
　Bushes are colored with flowers;
And the miracle of this great earth
　Awakens with fresh April showers.

Easter, the time of renewal,
　Easter, the time of great cheer,
Easter, the great resurrection
　Unfolds in spring of each year.

HOLY WEEK

Helen Kitchell Evans

The symbol of Holy Week is the cross;
　It speaks to us of Calvary,
And how our Savior died
　To save sinners like you and me.

It speaks of vile passions,
　Of envies, hatreds, and fears,
And all of the lusts of mankind
　That have lived these many years.

The Christ who hung upon the cross
　Only answered with love;
Love that suffered and endured,
　Love that triumphed from above.

I LOVE TO TELL THE STORY

Nona Keen Duffy

I love to tell the story
  Of Jesus and His birth,
Of how our blessed Lord was born
  And lived upon this earth!
I tell the manger story
  Where angels came to sing,
Of how the Wise-men sought His crib,
  Their richest gifts to bring!

He healed the sick and crippled,
  He made the blind to see,
He taught His twelve disciples much
  About their ministry!
He taught unselfish living
  And love for all things good;
He told us we are sons of God,
  Ennobling brotherhood.

He taught that love for brother
  Is greater than a crown,
Whether he be rich or poor,
  Or white or black or brown!
He told us it is just and right
  For everyone to give;
He set a fine example, too,
  Of how we are to live.

I love to tell the story
  Of how He died for men,
Of how He broke the bonds of death
  To rise and walk again!
I tell the Easter story
  Of how He rose above,
Of how He taught us how to live,
  And fill our hearts with love!

THE BEAUTY OF THE EARTH

Helen Kitchell Evans

The lovely flowers of the field
  Are so beautiful to see;
They tell us God is everywhere
  And alive for you and me.

Flowers planted near the church
  Show the beauty of creation;
They make us feel proud
  For our church and for the nation.

For the beauty of the earth
  We are thankful Easter Day;
May we always keep it so
  Is the prayer we pray.

Reading

THE PROMISE

by Clark Campbell

A monologue

Morning light streams through the high window. "No!" Half gasping, half crying, I try to hold back the sun. I sit crouched in a corner staring at a bright expanse of light. "Go away!" I watch, horrified, transfixed. The beam of light itself is visible, dust swirling through it. I close my eyes. My mind is frozen, yet races. Today. TODAY! I look wildly around my cell. Rough-hewn granite. Trails of water beneath the barred window. Coarse gray cloth pad against one wall. A bucket in the corner. Bare. Cold. No way out.

My gaze settles on the door. Heavy cedar. Aged. Brown. Small window. I can't look away. Soon it will open, and ... "No!" The cry echoes through the cell. Silence returns slowly. My gaze drops to my feet. Bare feet on a bare earth floor. Earth. "Dust thou art and to dust thou shalt return." The phrase from my childhood looms in my memory. The Pharisees used it every Sabbath. I never paid any attention. But now ... my mind drifts ...

"Simon, listen to your papa! He only wants ..."

"No, Mother. I will not! What do those priests know of us? Parading around with their fine robes, making a big fuss, giving a shekel here, a minim there. Why should I listen to them? Or to you, either? You just sit there, accept it, saying 'The Lord knows best.' Is there no room for the Lord to love? I'm leaving. Now."

"Simon, come back." Her harsh, pleading voice recedes. My eyes are still staring at the floor. Had I known then what I know now ... too late. Always too late. Too late to say, "I'm sorry." Or, "I've learned. I won't do it again." Too late to plead for life, when you are sentenced to die. Tears splash to the floor. "God, where are You now? Yes, I was wrong." I raise my face and then stand, raging at the ceiling. Begging. But what good does it do? Nobody listens. Anger spent, I fall back in the corner. I hear steps. The door shakes and opens. "No," I whisper.

Two Roman soldiers enter. They walk through the beam of light. It shines off their leather and armor. They stop, faces expressionless, hands on their sword hilts. "Come, Simon." Their hands take my arms and lift. "No," I plead. "No!" Fight. Don't let them take me. Their hands are strong—too strong. I'm pulled from the cell. My resistance drains. The cross lays before me. Dimly, as in a dream, I notice the crowd of people shouting and cursing. My mind and body are numb. A whip cracks. It strikes. "Carry it!" the soldiers shout. I obey. My shoulder is under the beam. Its weight presses down. Rough, splinters. Moments of time stand out. The narrow dirt road. Struggling uphill. Weight dragging. A child points at me and laughs. "Robber. Thief!" Curses rain down. Step. Another step. Golgotha. Place of the Skull. The top. I collapse. Hands roughly turn me over. Rope burns on my wrists and ankles. Pain. The nails enter crushing flesh and bones. PAIN. Movement. The cross is raised and dropped into place. "Ah-h-h."

Pain. All-consuming, never-ceasing pain. I can't breathe! Only by raising myself, pushing with my legs, can I breathe. If I rest, I can't breathe. Struggle! Live!

Dimly, I hear people shouting, "King, save yourself." "We're waiting, O King. Where are the angels?" I turn. Ten feet away there's another cross. Another man. King? A wooden plaque is over His head. "The King of the Jews." King? Who is He? He looks quiet, peaceful. Dying. No anger, only sorrow. "Come on, Jesus, save us." There is another criminal on a third cross.

Struggling, I focus on the middle cross. King of the Jews? Hoarsely, I cry, "Hey, I'm a Jew. Save me." No response. "Come on, King!" I spit the word. Anger consumes me. Pain, always pain. Jesus turns His head and looks at me. For a moment, the agony disappears. I've never seen eyes like that. Sorrow-filled, pain-filled, but strong and caring—even here. I turn away. My legs collapse. I can't breathe! Pain. Push with the legs. "Ohhh..." Breathing again. Those eyes are not of a man. I look back. He is speaking softly, looking down. "Father, forgive them. They don't know what they are doing." Father? I follow His gaze. Soldiers are below the cross. Forgive them? But they're *killing* us! My mind reels. How? How can He forgive them? How?

The crowd is roaring. Pharisees and priests are below the middle cross—His cross—taunting and angering the crowd. They have no compassion. The other criminal cries out cursing. Meaningless words. Terror, horror-filled words. The Pharisees and criminals are speaking the same words. Angry and horrible. Pain.

Almost wearily, a thought surfaces. King of the Jews? The prophet Isaiah wrote, "Led as a lamb to the slaughter." I struggle to remember. Who was he writing about? King of the Jews? Messiah? Suddenly, I remember. The Son of God. Messiah. Something pushes it back and tries to hide it. No! There is too much pain. I can't go on. God, help me! I live.

The cursing is continuing. I can't handle this. "Stop!" I scream. I glare, angrily, pleadingly, at the other criminal. "We deserve to be here. We're guilty, condemned." I close my eyes, open them again. My lips are dry. "But He isn't. He doesn't deserve this. He's done nothing wrong. Can't you see?" I close my eyes. Pain. I can't breathe. My legs are getting weaker. Push up! I look at Jesus. "Remember me. Remember, when you come into Your kingdom." He watches me. His voice is peaceful. "Today you'll be with me in paradise."

It is noon and blackness falls. There are earthquakes. The taunting and pain continues. Ignore it. The promise lingers. Believe it. Believe Him. Stillness falls. Jesus speaks. "My God, why have You forsaken me?" Silence. Again, His voice. "It is finished." No! Jesus is dead. "Help me," I silently cry.

Remember the promise. Believe it. Soldiers come and go over to the other criminal. They raise their clubs and break his legs. He can't lift himself--he can't breathe! They head for me. No! Remember the promise. Believe it! The clubs fall.

Exercises

BEAUTIFUL THINGS OF SPRING

Helen Kitchell Evans

All: The world is so filled with beautiful things:

1st Child: The flowering trees,

2nd Child: The bird that sings,

3rd Child: The sky of blue,

4th Child: The clouds on high,

5th Child: And sometimes a rainbow fills the sky.

All: The world is so filled with beautiful things:

6th Child: The sounds of joy that laughter brings,

7th Child: The church bells we hear on a special day When people gather to listen and pray.

All: The world is so filled with beautiful things:

8th Child: The flowers of the field,

9th Child: The grapevine that swings.

10th Child: Only God could give such joy to the earth.

All: Today let's give thanks for His glorious birth!

NEW BIRTH

Helen Kitchell Evans

Choir 1: He is real!

Choir 2: He is risen!

Chorus: The word to fulfill.

Choir 1: He is real!

Choir 2: He is risen!

Chorus: He is with us still.

Choir 1: He is real!

Choir 2: He is risen!

Chorus: To save us from sin.

Choir 1: He is real!

Choir 2: He is risen!

Chorus: The verdict is in.

Choir 1: He is real!

Choir 2: He is risen!

Chorus: The King of all earth.

Choir 1: He is real!

Choir 2: He is risen!

Chorus: To give us new birth.

IT IS SPRING

Helen Kitchell Evans

Choir 1: A little robin came today;

Choir 2: I heard his sweet voice ring.

Choir 1: His song was very cheery,

Choir 2: Above no clouds were dreary;

Chorus: And he sang and sang and sang, "It is Easter. It is spring."

Choir 1: This is what he said to me,

Choir 2: Oh my, how he did sing!

Solo 1: "Forget about the snow!

Solo 2: Forget north winds that blow!"

Chorus: And he sang and sang and sang, "It is Easter. It is spring."

HE IS RISEN

Helen Kitchell Evans

Leader: Let us welcome the King of Glory Who has risen from the tomb!

Congregation: He is risen! He is risen! Bless His holy name.

Leader: Let us welcome the Savior triumphant Who rolled the stone away!

Congregation: He is risen! He is risen! Bless His holy name.

Leader: Let us give glad acclaim For the Lord of life and glory!

Congregation: He is risen! He is risen! Bless His holy name.

Leader: Let us praise the victory That we celebrate today!

Congregation: He is risen! He is risen! Bless His holy name.

HEAR AND REJOICE

Helen Kitchell Evans

Choir 1: Lovely Easter lilies,

Choir 2: Can't you just hear what they tell?

Chorus: Ringing, ringing, ringing, *(Each word with more volume.)*

Solo: Full of joy is every church bell.

Choir 1: They bring us news from Heaven;

Choir 2: Listen to each special voice;

Choir 1: Hear their message everyone!

Choir 2: Hear, oh hear, and rejoice!

Chorus: See the lilies, hear the chimes, Christ is risen for all time!

EASTER SERVICE FOR THE PRIMARY DEPARTMENT

by Helen Kitchell Evans

(The children are arranged in choir formation. The entire service is presented from their position in the group.)

Recitation: "Prayer for Easter"

> We are thankful to You for Easter,
> For Jesus in Heaven today,
> For Jesus who taught us right,
> For Jesus to whom we pray.
> We are thankful for the sunshine,
> For the flowers and the birds that sing;
> We thank, You, for our parents, too,
> Thank You for everything.

Song: "After Prayer"

Recitation: "This Easter"

> This Easter I am happy
> Because the Spring is here;
> I want to say "Hello" to you,
> And bring you Easter cheer.

Song: "Spring Has Come"

Recitation: "This World"

> This wonderful world was made
> For you and me;
> It's a lovely place
> For us to be.

Song: "All Things Beautiful"

Recitation: "I Like Stars"

> I like the stars up in the sky,
> The stars that twinkle light;
> They make me think of Jesus
> When I see them at night.

Song: "I Will Give Thanks"

Exercise: "For All"

> **All:** This wonderful world was made for all,
> **Solo 1:** Let us keep it clean and pure;
> **Solo 2:** I know that Jesus wants us to,
> Of that I am quite sure.
> **Solo 3:** Let us make the world a better place
> For having lived right here.
> **All:** Let us try to think of others
> And spread God's love and cheer.

Song: "It Was Good"

Offering Recitation:

> Now we will receive
> Our offering for this day;
> We know to spread God's Word
> We must help in this way.

Offering (music played during collection)

Benediction Recitation: "May God Be With Us"

> May God be with all of us today,
> And go with us and with us stay,
> In Jesus' name, we humbly pray.

Benediction Song

ALL THINGS BEAUTIFUL

Words by Helen Kitchell Evans
Based on John 1:3; Ecc. 3:11

Music by Frances Mann Benson

He hath made ev-ery-thing beau - ti -ful,

In His time, In His time. All things were made by

Him,___ In His time, In His time.

BENEDICTION

2 Corinthians 13:14

Music by Frances Mann Benson

The love of God be with___ us all.

SPRING HAS COME

Words by Helen Kitchell Evans

Music by Frances Mann Benson

The flow-ers ap-pear on the earth___ For, lo, the win-ter is past,___ The time of the sing-ing of birds has come, has come at last.___ The ten-der grass show-eth it-self,___ 'Tis spring, spring, spring.___ For, lo, the win-ter is

past, ____ It is spring, spring, spring. ____

AFTER PRAYER

Psalm 34:1; 46:1

Frances Mann Benson

I will bless the Lord   at all   times,   I will

praise him ev - ery day;   He · is my strength when I

need Him, He   lis - tens when-ev - er I   pray.

IT WAS GOOD

Words by Helen Kitchell Evans
Based on Gen. 1:25

Music by Frances Mann Benson

God made the love - ly world we see, He made the nice green leaves; He made the stars to shine at night, He made the beau - ti - ful trees; When God looked at the world He made He saw that it was good, And He hopes all boys and

girls_____ will care for it as they should._____

I WILL GIVE THANKS

Words by Helen Kitchell Evans   Music by Frances Mann Benson
Based on Psalm 9:1a, 136:7a, 136:8a, 136:9a

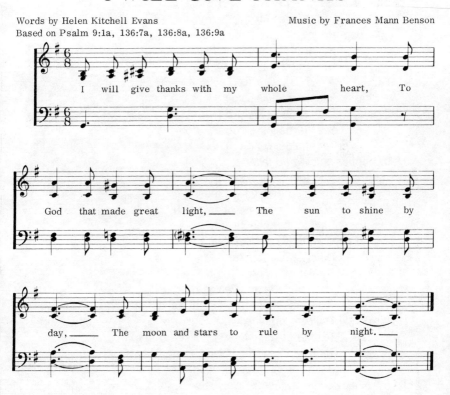

I will give thanks with my whole heart, To

God that made great light,_____ The sun to shine by

day,_____ The moon and stars to rule by night._____

SHARE THE STORY

Velda Blumhagen

A program of recitations for children

Directions: Eleven Primary children enter carrying large cut-out letters, G-O, T-E-A-C-H, H-E-A-L. They all sing the song and then take turns speaking.

Song *(sung to tune of "Jesus Loves Me"):*
Jesus loves us, this is true;
He loves other people ,too.
He wants us to go and share
News of Jesus everywhere.

Chorus: Yes, Jesus loves you.
Yes, Jesus loves you.
Yes, Jesus loves you.
The Bible says it's true.

First child *(holding up letter "G"):*
God told us in His Word,
Into all the world we must go
With the message of salvation,
Until all the people know.

Second child *(holding up letter "O"):*
Others need to hear
The story we have to give.
Eternal life is for everyone
Who for Jesus is willing to live.

Third child *(holding up letter "T"):*
Tell the gospel story
That God sent His only Son
Because He loves the world,
And that means everyone!

Fourth child *(holding up letter "E"):*
Everyone is important;
And we must live each day

With the help of God the Father
In a pure, Christ-like way.

Fifth child *(holding up letter "A"):*
All things with God are possible,
We read in His holy Word.
He wants us to teach the Bible story
Until everyone has heard.

Sixth child *(holding up letter "C"):*
"Come unto me"—
This is Jesus' call.
To you, and you, and me,
Jesus says, "Come all."

Seventh child *(holding up letter "H"):*
Hear the voice of God
As He calls each one today,
To come and live for Him
In God's own loving way.

Eighth child *(holding up letter "H"):*
Help the brokenhearted,
The hurt and sick and lame.
Missionary doctors and nurses
Bring healing in Jesus' name.

Ninth child *(holding up letter "E"):*
Each one of us can help
All those who are in need,
By giving of our blessings,
Or doing a kind deed..

Tenth child *(holding up letter "A"):*
All we ask for in prayer,
Believing, we shall receive.
Go, teach, and heal,
And on God's Word believe.

Eleventh child *(holding up letter "L"):*
"Love others," said Jesus,
"As I have loved each of you."
Giving this message of love
Is what God wants us to do.

All *(repeating in unison with letters held high):*
"Go and make disciples of all nations ... and surely I will be with
you always, to the very end of the age.

As the children leave the platform, an older choir sings "We've a
Story to Tell to the Nations."

Mother's Day

I REMEMBER

James A. Brown

I remember the days we sat and
talked
  While sharing a laugh or two;
You told me many important things—
  I should have listened to you.

I remember you in the kitchen
  Cooking my favorite meal;
You showed me a love I couldn't un-
derstand,
  A love that was special and real.

I remember watching you work so
hard,
  You scrubbed and cleaned with
  your hands;
If I had only worked half as hard,
  I'd have been a better man.

I remember the rides we used to take;
  I had no worries or cares.
Now I would give anything
  To ride or just be there.

I remember the times you gave me
your last
  Because you didn't want me to be
  without;
You really must have loved me,
  How could I have any doubt?

Yes, many days have passed since
then;
  There have been many Januarys
  and Decembers.
I'm writing this poem to let you know
  I love you and I remember!

NOW THAT I'M A MOTHER

Debra Jessup

Appreciation is what I learned so late
in life;
It took a child of my own and being a
wife.
I can still remember the cry from behind my mother's closed door
Because of something I'd said or
done that made her feel I just
wanted more.
I remember my father saying, "Please
be nice to your mother.
The things she does for you she'd do
for no other."
So many times she longed to hear a
remark of approval,
Something she never knew until the
time of removal.
A phone call is the way we keep in
touch these days;
The many hugs I took for granted I
wish I could have back in so many
ways.
I see her a few times a year,
And mother is now a name I truly hold
dear.
Happy Mother's Day, Grandmother,
Mother, and friend.

34

A GOOD PAL

Agnes Finch Whitacre

Your mother is a friend to you;
Her tender love is ever true.
She watches with such tender care
And guides and guards with every
    prayer.
She knows when you are really
    troubled,
And then her worries, too, are
    doubled.
When you are sick, she feels sad too,
But seems to know just what to do
To make you better, ease the pain,
And help you to feel well again.
So just remember: There's no other
Better friend than your mother!

PLEASING MOTHER

Grayce Boller

Mothers work harder than we know
    For their children each day;
We should do the best we can
    To ease their rugged way.

It will please them, if at home
    We'd do an extra chore;
And if we mind the things they say,
    Nothing would please them more.

Better work at home and school
    And kind things that we do,
Would make our mothers happy,
    And make us happier, too!

SO DEAR

Agnes Finch Whitacre

How grateful can a daughter be
    For such a mother and dad?
You've given me the nicest things
    A daughter ever had.
A home with tender loving care,
    Fulfilled my every need;
Your thoughtfulness, encouragement,
    Inspired me to succeed.
You, Mother, are always there
    To lend an open ear;
And, Dad, on you I can depend—
    You both to me are dear!

JESUS AND MOTHER

Grayce Boller

Jesus and Mother, the two that I love,
Blessings to me from the Father
    above.
Doing their will and bringing them joy,
There's no greater wish for a girl or a
    boy.

Jesus was good to His mother, I know,
And in Jesus' way I want to go.
Good to my mother I always will be,
Because of the things that she does
    for me.

Knowing my Lord is filled with delight,
Seeing me help her by day and by
    night;
Knowing my mother is made happy,
    too,
Help me to please her in all that I do.

STEPMOTHER

Jewel Ballay

I never knew my mother, the one who
    gave me birth,
But I've been told she ranked among
    the greatest of the earth.
So proud I am to hear those words,
    but I've a tribute too,
For one who's given me her love and
    saw me safely through.

No mother ever sacrificed or gave a
    love so free
As my stepmother sacrificed and
    gave her love to me.
I think it's time a tribute's due to one
    who's filled a need,
Someone who's given of herself un-
    mindful of her deed.

I often think how hard she worked—
    the skill she did employ,
In fashioning a lovely dress that
    brought me boundless joy.
I can't forget how, through the years,
    she loved me as her own,
And on each Mother's Day I feel our
    love has stronger grown.

I'm very sure somehow, somewhere, a
    mother understands,
And is so glad her child had care from
    another's loving hands.

THE HOMELESS CHILDREN

Rega Kramer McCarty

There are many orphaned children
    In near and far-off lands
Who do not have a mother
    Who loves and understands.

There are children of every nation,
    Who feel alone and lost;
I think we should try to help them,
    Whatever be the cost.

We should feel truly thankful
    That we have a mother's love;
And remember they, too, are children
    Of our Heavenly Father above!

MOTHERS ARE SPECIAL

E. Gano Karns

Mothers are a special gift
    That God has given us;
They teach us how to study,
    They teach us how to trust.

They show us that God loves us,
    They teach us how to pray;
They feed and clothe and care for us
    Each and every day.

They say that we must always
    Thank God for everything
That He gives to us daily,
    Our happiness to bring.

I'm sure there is no other
    To remind us every day
That we should live for Jesus
    And always walk His way.

MAY IS FOR MOTHERS

Grace Clark

I'm glad that Mother's special day
Comes in the flow'ry month of May,
When lilacs wave their purple plumes,
And tulips add their sweet perfumes.

Each mother, whether young or old,
Gives gifts far more precious than
  gold;
Like roses' fragrance, she gives love
Unmatched, except by God above.

REMEMBERED MELODIES

Mabel Hill

Long years have passed, but I can
  hear
  As in the long ago,
A tender melody that mother sang
  So soft and low;
"Rock of ages, cleft for me,
  Let me hide myself in Thee."
In fancy I'm a child
  And mother bends above my bed;
How tenderly she smoothed the hair
  That curled around my head.

Once more I find a peace
  In that old, sacred melody,
Such joy it brought me
  When my mother sang to me,
"Rock of ages, cleft for me,
  Let me hide myself in Thee."
Dear Lord, I now cling to You
  As Mother in that day;
Her faith has brought me here,
  And humbly at Thy cross I pray,
"Rock of ages, cleft for me,
  Let me hide myself in Thee."

LOVE MEANS MOST

Lois Anne Williams

You could kiss my scrapes and
  bumps,
  And chase the pain away;
You could solve those problems
  That come into my day.

You could always lend a hand
  When my task was too much;
You could handle every chore
  With your own special touch.

But what means the most to me
  Is all the love you share;
It is good to have a mother
  Who gives such loving care.

GOD'S HIGHEST CALLING

Ada Tomlinson

God calls some to preach His Word,
  Some others He calls to sing;
Some people are called to little tasks,
  And others to a greater thing.
I'm sure when He called you to
  motherhood
  And watched that baby grow,
He chose the highest calling of all
  For mothers to have, I know!

MY MOTHER'S EYES

Deta Lasley

My mother's eyes are soft and brown
    (blue)
    And shiny as a penny.
She loves me very much, I know;
    Her kindnesses are many.

My mother's eyes are loving,
    With tender gazes warm.
She leads me on life's pathway
    And shelters me from harm.

My mother's eyes are searching;
    They uncover hidden snares.
She shoulders every burden
    And lightens all my cares.

My mother's eyes are hurtful
    When I'm going through a test;
She tries to take the pain away;
    She always knows what's best.

My mother's eyes are beautiful,
    God sent them from above.
I know that this is true because
    I can see in them His love.

DISPLAY OF MOTHER LOVE

Jewel Ballay

Beneath the cross she knelt and
    prayed
    For Christ, who did no wrong.
Beneath the cross He saw her there,
    His mother, brave and strong.

Her work-worn hands and saddened
    face,
    Her shoulders bent with care.
Beneath His cross she prayed for Him,
    While bathed in deep despair.

The Master knew a mother's love
    As mother's love should be,
A wondrous act of sacrifice
    Displayed so tenderly.

There is no blessing that exceeds
    A mother's precious love.
The hand that rocks the cradle is
    A gift from God above.

On Mother's Day let hearts rejoice
    And once again recall
That Mary was the choice of God,
    The greatest mother of all.

A FINE EXAMPLE

Ada Tomlinson

If daughters are like their mothers,
    Then I am lucky indeed;
For Mom is a good example
    And her teachings I'll heed.
I am sure if I resemble
    Her god-like ways I see,
I'll be a fine example
    For my own children to be.

MOTHER'S FLOWER

Effie Crawford

When summer comes to greet us,
   There are many lovely flowers
That grow along the roadside
   And bloom in leafy bowers.

The lilies and the roses
   We watch and tend with care;
They flourish in their beauty,
   And fragrance fills the air.

But there's a dainty flower
   We cherish as no other;
The delicate carnation—
   It's especially for Mother.

WE SAY THANK YOU

Ada Tomlinson

1st Child
For your loving care for me each day
   I say, "Thank you."

2nd Child
For your teaching me to read and pray
   I say, "Thank you."

3rd Child
For nourishing me since I was born
   I say, "Thank you."

4th Child
For taking me to church on Sunday
   morn
   I say, "Thank you."

All:
For all the mothers here today,
   Your love and care amazes,
We thank you from our hearts
Because you're worthy of our praises.

SUPER, SUPER MOM

Nancy Bell

1st Child:
Mothers are special;
   They're always nearby.
They never stop loving,
   And here are some reasons why.

2nd Child:
Mothers are generous,
   They always have a kiss;
And when we go away sometimes,
   They're the very first ones we miss.

3rd Child:
My mother plays with me,
   And will seldom refuse,
And I know she loves me
   Whether I win or lose.

4th Child:
My mother sometimes scolds me
   And uses the "rod,"
To show me and teach me
   To love and obey God.

5th Child:
My mother says I'm special
   Though sometimes I'm bad;
She forgives me and hugs me,
   And makes me feel glad.

6th Child:
Mother knows about Jesus,
   Maybe that's why she's so good;
I wish all mothers were Christians,
   Teaching boys and girls as they
   should.

7th Child:
For all these things and many more
   This day we celebrate;
For we each have a mother
   Who is super, super great!

MOTHERS ARE WONDERFUL

Alice Stewart

All:
Mothers are wonderful!

1st Child:
Mothers are wonderful;
Day after day
They teach us and guide us
In the right way.

2nd Child:
Mothers are wonderful;
If we are sad
They know what to say
To make us feel glad.

3rd Child:
Mothers are wonderful;
Giving and sharing,
Gentle and true,
Loving and caring.

4th Child:
Mothers are wonderful;
They always know
Just how to help us
As older we grow.

5th Child:
Mothers are wonderful;
Tender and kind,
All that we need
In Mother we find.

All:
Mothers are wonderful!

WHAT ARE MOMS FOR?

Eleanor Pankow

1st Child
Mothers are for helping us
Just as they should.
Mothers are for showing us
How to be good.

2nd Child
Mothers are for teaching us
Of Jesus' love,
And of God, our dear Father
In Heaven above.

3rd Child
Mothers are for loving
And helping each day,
For they love and help us
On all of life's way.

EVERY DAY

Margaretta Harmon

1st Child

(Holds calendar page for May and points to the date of Mother's Day.)

The calendar says today's the day
To honor our mothers a special way.

2nd Child

(Points to other dates.)
I think you'll agree with me when I say
That every day should be Mother's Day.

WHAT MOTHER'S DAY MEANS

Velda Blumhagen

1st Child
What does it mean to honor mothers
  And for children to obey?
Why do we like to celebrate
  A special Mother's Day?

2nd Child
Honor means to have respect,
  To show good manners, too.
It means being thoughtful of Mother
  And helpful in all we do.

3rd Child
Honor means obeying,
  Or doing what Mother asks;
It means being glad and willing
  To do our chores and tasks.

4th Child
We like to give honor to mothers
  On this special day in May;
But let us also obey and honor
  Our mothers on *every* day.

MOTHER'S DAY IS EVERY DAY

Rega Kramer McCarty

1st Child
Mother's Day is every day,
  For only through her love
Do I know Jesus, my Savior,
  Who watches from above.

2nd Child
Mother's Day is every day,
  For only through her care
Do I know the Bible stories
  And the helpfulness of prayer.

3rd Child
Mother's Day is every day,
  And every girl and boy
Can truly thank a mother
  For the blessings they enjoy.

A BASKET OF THANKS

Velda Blumhagen

(For five children; the fifth stands at center with shallow basket.)

1st Child
Thank you, Mother, for kindness
  In things you do and say.
Thank you for teaching me always
  In a kind and loving way.
(Puts flower in basket.)

2nd Child
Thank you, Mother, for helping
  With hard things I must do,
Helping me to choose the right,
  And forgiving wrong things, too.
(Puts flower in basket.)

3rd Child
Thank you, Mother, for comfort
  When I'm hurt or am not well;
I'm glad you always listen
  To the troubles that I tell.
(Puts flower in basket.)

4th Child
We bring our thanks to Mother
  On this her special day;
But we should also show our thanks
  In things we do and say.
(Puts flower in basket, then fifth child presents basket to a mother.)

41

OUR RESOLVE

Rega Kramer McCarty

1st Child

Are we always careful
  To say the things we should?
To tell our mothers when the cake
  She bakes is very good?

2nd Child

Do we remember always
  To thank her for her care,
Or help her with the many tasks
  Which we should gladly share?

3rd Child

Do we try to please her,
  Or must we all confess
That if we were more thoughtful
  We would bring her happiness?

All

We will make a resolution
  Upon this Mother's Day;
We shall try to be more thoughtful
  In all we do and say!

BEST GIFT

Rega Kramer McCarty

Child

(Carries picture he has drawn.)

I brought you a present, Mother,
  Because it is Mother's Day;
I want you to know I love you
  In every single way!

It isn't a very big present,
  I made it in school this week,
But before I let you have it,
  Please, Mother, turn your cheek!
(Mother does so and Child kisses her.)

Mother

Whatever your gift is, honey,
  There's nothing as nice as this;
Mothers love more than anything
  A sweet and loving kiss.

Let me see what you made me—
(Child hands Mother picture.)
  O what a lovely sheet!
A picture you've drawn all by your-
    self—
  What a thoughtful treat!

How sweet of you to remember,
  And how your eyes do shine!
But what makes me the happiest
  Is knowing that you are mine!

MOTHER, I LOVE YOU

Carolyn Scheidies

(Dark except for spotlight on performers. Mother is reading a story to three young children at her feet.)

1st Child

Mother, I love you
 When you care for me each day.
I love you when you read to me
 Or walk beside me on the way.

(Mother and children kneeling beside small bed or cot.)

2nd Child

Mother, you make me happy
 As together we kneel to pray,
As you teach me of Jesus' love
 In whatever you do and say.

(Children hug Mother and leave one at a time until one child remains.)

3rd Child

Mother, today I thank you
 For all the love you've shown;
Because of you, I too, will love
 My children when I am grown.

NO FANCY WORDS

Dorothy Stroud

1st Child

We don't have any fancy words
 To help us tell you we adore
The mothers God has given us;
 We simply couldn't love them more!

2nd Child

They've cared for us so tenderly
 Since we were very small;
They sew, and cook, and clean all day
 And never ask for thanks at all.

3rd Child

They've taught us how to act and talk,
 But best of all, to truly pray,
And how to trust our loving Lord
 To guide us safely day by day.

4th Child

They've read the Bible to us since
 We could begin to understand
That we can only be content
 When we obey our Lord's commands.

5th Child

God was so very good to give us
 Christian mothers, sweet and fine;
But if you'd ask each one of us,
 We'd say, "The dearest one is mine!"

All

We don't need fancy words to say
"We love you, Mom, in every way!"

Father's Day

WELCOME

Hazel Bacon

We are very glad
Because of this day.
Welcome to all fathers
Who are here today.

HONOR MY FATHER

Rega Kramer McCarty

I'm glad that this is Father's Day;
Honor to him I shall show,
For my father is the finest man
A boy could ever know!

I'M GLAD

Hazel Bacon

Dad, I'm glad to have you here;
We like to share with you.
I love to hear your stories,
And see good things you do.

A TIME TO HONOR DAD

Esther Johnson

*(To be given in unison by two or three
small boys.)*

It's time to honor all dads now;
So here's a tribute and a bow.
*(Boys make a big bow before the
audience.)*

I KNOW

Hazel Bacon

I know about my father;
He is big, strong, and good.
He teaches me the right things,
Just as a father should.

A FATHER'S DAY WELCOME

Margaretta Harmon

Though I am small,
(hold hand over head)
I still can say,
(cup hands to mouth)
Welcome, dads!
(spread both arms wide)
It's *your* day!
(point to audience)

DEAR DAD

Hazel Bacon

(Holds up letter.)
I have written you this letter
To tell more about my love.
Thank you for working hard for us;
I'm sure God knows, from above.

BLESS US ALL

Mary Howard Poole

I know I'm just a little boy,
But old enough to say,
God bless my own loving dad,
And all dads here today.

I WOULD LIKE

Hazel Bacon

I would like to sing a song
  For my daddy to enjoy,
But it has to be a short one
  Because I'm not a singing boy.
(May sing a song.)

IT'S FITTING

Rega Kramer McCarty

It's fitting we should have this day
Set aside for Dad;
To pay him honor well deserved
Makes us mighty glad!

DAD

Eleanor Pankow

(Boy carries paper scroll with "DAD" in capitals.)

Two letters in the alphabet
  I need to spell out "Dad."
And mine's the best, the very best
  A son has ever had.

JUST WANT TO SAY

Rega Kramer McCarty

Hey, Dad, I just want to say,
Happy, happy Father's Day!

A LOVING DAD

Alexander Seymour

Do you know why I am glad?
Well, I have a loving dad.
He is kind to Mother and me;
That's why I'm glad, you see.

WELCOME

Ruth Spurling

"Welcome, today,"
To you we say.
We are so glad
For every dad.

MY DAD

Ralphine Jacobs

My dad is the greatest
That there could ever be.
How do I know
That this is so?
That's the way he is to me.

YOUR WAY

Ruth Spurling

Welcome to you, fathers,
  For this is your day.
We'll be especially nice to you
  And do things your way.

HONOR FOR GRANDFATHERS

Agnes Finch Whitacre

I'm glad there's now
  A day set aside
To honor all the grandfathers
  In whom we can confide.
They seem to have a special place
  For growing girls and boys,
Because they listen, share, and talk,
  And mend their broken toys.
When troubles come, as come they
    will,
  They know just what to say;
They never scold, but love us more,
  Then troubles melt away!

LAST YEAR
Hazel Bacon

Last year I was so little
I didn't know my line.
Today I can remember;
This welcome is—all mine.

GOD MADE FATHERS
Ruth Otto

I think God must have made fathers
To help hold families together,
Using divine guidance and wisdom
Through fair and stormy weather.

Fathers are really important
Today, as they were long ago;
Every family ought to have one
To help the children to grow.

A family isn't really complete
Without a father strong and true,
Being faithful to God and country,
Doing the best he knows how to do.

God bless all you wonderful fathers
Who walk with God all the way.
You're a blessing to those who love
you;
We wish you joy and gladness today.

MY GRANDPA
Agnes Finch Whitacre

I have a grandpa who understands,
And tries to do all that he can
To help me in the game of life,
To face each day of joy and strife.
He takes the time to play with me,
And then explains so I will see
That fate will never make me lose,
But God's right way I must choose!

NO GREATER JOY
Jewel Ballay

If I could spend one hour again upon
my daddy's knee,
I'd hear his hearty laugh and know his
tender love for me;
If I could feel his hand clasp mine in
his protecting way,
I could not ask a greater joy upon this
Father's Day.

If I could look into his eyes and see
reflected there
Such pride as only God can give for
something rich and rare;
If I could hear him speak once more
in his inspiring way,
I could not ask a greater joy upon this
Father's Day.

A FATHER'S DAY PRAYER
Jewel Ballay

Dear Father, hear my humble plea:
Be merciful, I pray,
To all good men who share the joy
Of fatherhood today.

Give them the strength and needed
skill
Their missions to attain;
And give them courage to press on
When life would seem in vain.

Dear Master, on this Father's Day,
With Your abiding love:
Remind us, God, our Father lives
And watches from above.

FROM DAD

Jewel Ballay

Upon this Father's Day, dear Lord,
    hear my humble prayer
That faith and trust will fill the hearts
    of fathers everywhere.
May they seek Thy wondrous love to
    guide them on their way,
And know that pride and joy is theirs
    upon this Father's Day.

A FATHER SPEAKS

Mary Jenkin

I'm my boy's hero, this I know;
He thinks I'm tops, and tells me so.
He likes to keep me in his sight;
Whate'er I do is always right!

And though worthy I try to be,
Sometimes it almost frightens me.
I hope I'll never do or say
Something to lead my boy astray.

I'll ask God's help so I may guide
This youngster walking at my side.
This is my goal, to help him be
The kind of boy God wants to see.

The Lord God wants our love,
And asks fathers of today
To do His will whatever it be;
But most of all, to pray.

To seek His guidance and receive
The blessings He can give,
A heart that's full of thankfulness
As for Him we daily live.

PROUD OF DAD

Deta Lasley

There are many kinds of fathers,
    Every kind from A to Z;
But the very best of fathers
    Is the one who belongs to me.
He isn't always smiling,
    But it takes a lot to fade
That effervescent smile
    That he has from day to day.

If anybody needs some help,
    He's always there to give.
He'll help in any way he can
    And tries real hard to live
A life that God approves of,
    So you know he's pretty good.
But I begin to wonder when
    He tells of his childhood!

I guess you'd say that father
    Is no different from the rest;
But just because he's what he is,
    He's the father I love best!

EVENING RITUAL

Ruth Ebberts

Now the evening chores are done,
    The tasks he loves to do,
And now a quiet time has come
    When the busy day is through.
In his chair beside the fire,
Father (Grandpa) starts his reading
In the book of Psalms, where Christ
    Is Lord and shepherd, leading.
Hands, work-worn and gnarled with
    age,
Rest reverently upon the page.

47

FATHER'S GIFT

Ruth Otto

Father knows how to give gifts,
  Whatever the occasion may be.
It may be a book for my brother,
  Or a box of candy for me.

Father knows how to give advice;
  With wisdom he weighs each word.
He knows how to deliver a message;
  He's the best teacher I've ever heard.

The best gift that Dad ever gave
  Was the news the Jesus loves me;
That to give me life forever
  Jesus died on Calvary.

The best advice that Dad gave me
  Was to acknowledge God's love;
To live each day to its fullest,
  Walking with the Father above.

I believe that Dad himself was a gift,
  For God knew how wrong it would
  be
For families to live without fathers;
  That's why He gave Dad to me.

OUR WISHES

Rega Kramer McCarty

1st Child
I wish upon this Father's Day
  That you may be repaid
For every little sacrifice
  That you have gladly made!

2nd Child
I wish upon this Father's Day
  You receive your heart's desire;
Surely you deserve it
  For the courage you inspire!

3rd Child
I wish upon this Father's Day
Good health may come to you,
That you may find great happiness
  And all your dreams come true!

4th Child
Dear fathers, on this Father's Day
  We've wished you special joys;
We also bring our grateful love,
  From all your girls and boys!

A TRIBUTE TO FATHERS

Esther Johnson

1st Child
We'd like in some small measure
  To thank our dads today,
To say kind words of gratitude
  And honor him some way.

2nd Child
You may not have a million,
  Or be an astronaut,
But by your Christian living
  We all are being taught.

3rd Child
So thank you all, dear fathers,
  For teaching what is right,
For choosing the Bible
  To be your guiding light.